Earth

by Gina Dal Fuoco

Science Contributor
Sally Ride Science
Science Consultants
Nancy McKeown, Planetary Geologist
William B. Rice, Engineering Geologist

First hardcover edition published in 2009 by
Compass Point Books
151 Good Counsel Drive
P.O. Box 669
Mankato, MN 56002-0669

Editor: Jennifer VanVoorst
Designer: Heidi Thompson
Editorial Contributor: Sue Vander Hook

Art Director: LuAnn Ascheman-Adams
Creative Director: Joe Ewest
Editorial Director: Nick Healy
Managing Editor: Catherine Neitge

 This book was manufactured with paper containing at least 10 percent post-consumer waste.

Library of Congress Cataloging-in-Publication Data
Fuoco, Gina Dal.
  Earth / by Gina Dal Fuoco.
  p. cm. — (Mission: Science)
  Includes index.
  ISBN 978-0-7565-4070-8 (library binding)
  1. Earth—Juvenile literature. I. Title. II. Series.
  QB631.4.F86 2009
  333.72—dc22   2008037575

Visit Compass Point Books on the Internet at *www.compasspointbooks.com*
or e-mail your request to *custserv@compasspointbooks.com*

Table of Contents

What kind of home do you live in? Is it a house, a mobile home, an apartment—or maybe something else? Now imagine living there the rest of your life. You would make sure your home was a comfortable and pleasant place to live. If the walls, floor, or ceiling got damaged, you would fix them. You would make sure your home was stocked with an ample supply of healthy food and clean water to drink. And you would want the air you breathe to be fresh and pure.

Earth is also our home. It is home to billions of people and animals who will live on its land, in its waters, and in its air for the rest of their lives. It is the only home any of us will ever have. We want to take care of it—not just for ourselves, but also for the generations to come. If we are not careful with our planet, it may become damaged beyond repair or run out of the things we need to survive.

Did You Know?

Planet Earth has its own special holiday. Earth Day is celebrated every year on April 22. The holiday was first celebrated in 1970 as a way to bring attention to the growing environmental movement. Many important laws were passed by Congress in the wake of the 1970 Earth Day, including the Clean Air Act and the creation of the Environmental Protection Agency.

A Bird's Eye View

In 1983, Sally Ride became the first American woman to travel in space. In her space shuttle, which orbited 200 miles (322 kilometers) above Earth, she looked down from the stratosphere, through the atmosphere, and took pictures of Earth. Over the years, other astronauts have followed her lead. More than 350,000 color photos have been taken on space shuttle missions. Astronauts like Ride hope people learn a lot about Earth from their pictures.

Those who have seen Earth from space say the view helps them appreciate how fragile our world is and how important it is to protect it.

7

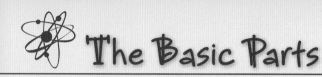

There are three basic parts, or systems, that make up our planet: the atmosphere, the hydrosphere, and the geosphere. Together they make up a larger system called the biosphere. We need to take good care of them all so they will last a very long time.

The atmosphere is like the ceiling and walls of our home. This huge outer layer of gases surrounds Earth and protects it from extreme temperatures. The atmosphere extends more than 90 miles (145 km) out from Earth's surface. But there's no real

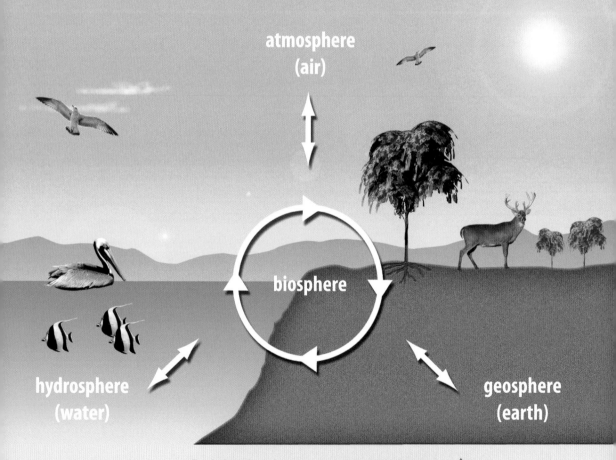

Earth has three important systems. Their interaction is part of a larger system called the biosphere.

Clouds are part of both the ⬆
atmosphere and the hydrosphere.

Did You Know?

Although the atmosphere is more than 90 miles (145 km) thick, most of the air is in the 25 miles (40 km) closest to Earth.

boundary where it ends. It keeps getting thinner and thinner until it fades into outer space.

Why is the atmosphere so important? It protects Earth from getting too much harmful radiation from the sun. At the same time, it holds in some of the sun's heat—ideally, just enough to keep everything at the right temperature. It also contains the air we breathe—a very important part of staying alive.

Another part of Earth is the hydrosphere. This system is made up of all the water on the planet. The hydrosphere includes oceans, lakes, rivers, and streams. It also includes the groundwater beneath Earth's surface and water vapor in the air. It includes snow and ice, as well as the water found in the soil. We can't survive without water—lots of clean, healthy water.

The third part is the geosphere—the solid parts of our planet. It is made up of rocks, mountains, pebbles, and sand. We can't see most of the geosphere because it's under the surface of the planet. But if we could see deep into the middle of Earth, we would see a solid inner core surrounded by a liquid outer core. The core is made up mostly of the element iron.

Many plants and animals make the hydrosphere their home.

Surrounding the core is the largest layer, the mantle. The crust is the layer closest to Earth's surface. The geosphere is like the foundation of a house, the strong structure that supports everything else.

The three parts of Earth—atmosphere, hydrosphere, and geosphere—all work together to maintain Earth as an ideal habitat for life. Can you imagine what life would be like if one of these parts were missing?

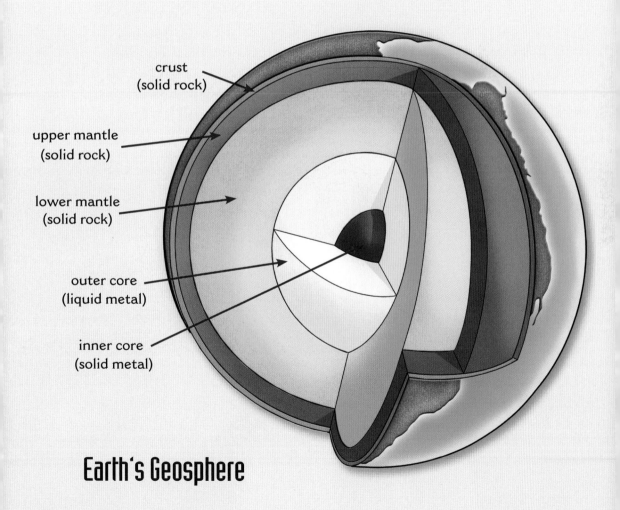

crust
(solid rock)

upper mantle
(solid rock)

lower mantle
(solid rock)

outer core
(liquid metal)

inner core
(solid metal)

Earth's Geosphere

Atmosphere: Keeping the Air Clean

Scientists have divided the atmosphere, the huge layer of air above us, into four layers: troposphere, stratosphere, mesosphere, and thermosphere. The lowest level, the troposphere, is the air where we live. It is where the clouds drift, the rain falls, and the wind blows. Air at the lowest part of the troposphere (nearest the ground) is the warmest. Air temperature drops as you go higher into the troposphere. That's why it's colder at the top of a mountain.

Warming the Planet

Earth needs warmth from the sun. First the sun's rays shine down through the atmosphere and hit Earth,

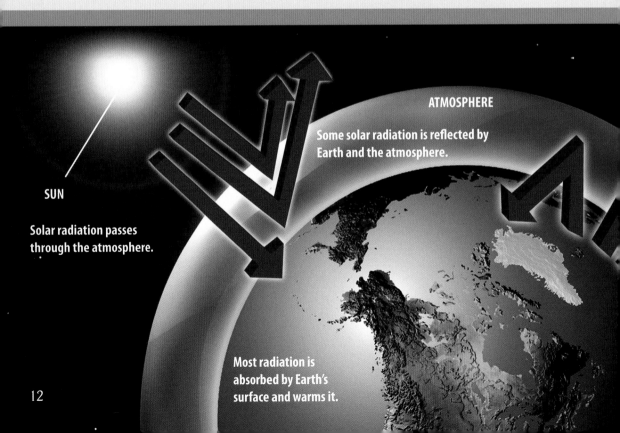

ATMOSPHERE

Some solar radiation is reflected by Earth and the atmosphere.

SUN

Solar radiation passes through the atmosphere.

Most radiation is absorbed by Earth's surface and warms it.

warming it up. Then some of the heat radiates back up and is released into outer space. Other heat is absorbed by gases such as carbon dioxide, water vapor, methane, and ozone. They trap the heat in our atmosphere so Earth is warm enough for us to live comfortably.

Gases that trap heat in the atmosphere have come to be called greenhouse gases. They cause Earth to warm up like the inside of a greenhouse in which plants are grown. In a greenhouse, the sun's rays shine through the glass ceiling and walls and warm up the inside air. The glass traps the heat inside.

Infrared radiation is emitted from Earth's surface.

Some of the infrared radiation passes through the atmosphere, and some is absorbed and re-emitted in all directions by greenhouse gas molecules. The effect of this is to warm Earth's surface and the lower atmosphere.

A Gaseous Mix

The atmosphere—or air—is made up of a mixture of mostly nitrogen and oxygen, with smaller concentrations of argon, carbon dioxide, and water vapor. Too much of any of these gases can cause harmful changes to our atmosphere.

The Problem With Greenhouse Gases

The process of the sun warming up Earth is normal. It is also normal for greenhouse gases to trap the heat in our atmosphere. But scientists say that too many greenhouse gases is not a good thing.

Many human activities also release greenhouse gases into the air. Some activities are as natural as breathing, which releases carbon dioxide.

Additional gases come from cars and trucks that emit gases from their tailpipes. Tall stacks at a manufacturing plant belch out gases. These gases are the same as the natural gases produced by nature—mostly carbon dioxide, methane, and ozone. But scientists warn that too many greenhouse gases in our atmosphere will trap too much heat, and Earth will get too warm.

Disappearing Animals

Pollution or global warming can cause an entire animal species to die. When that happens, the animal is considered to be extinct. Sometimes animals become extinct from natural causes. But other times human activities damage their habitat and endanger the species. Scientists are now watching the colorful harlequin frogs of Central and South America. Nearly two-thirds of the species has vanished since the 1980s. Many researchers believe that Earth's rising temperatures and changing climate are wiping them out.

Global Warming

The problem of Earth getting too warm is called global warming. The greenhouse gas that causes the most problem is carbon dioxide. The amount of carbon dioxide in the atmosphere has been increasing over the years.

The most significant increase occurred between 1973 and 2006. Scientists are advising people to work to limit the amount of carbon dioxide that goes into our air so too much heat is not trapped in the atmosphere.

Arctic Sea ice, 1979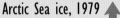

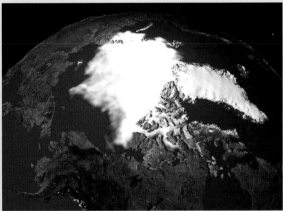

Arctic Sea ice, 2003

Predicting the Weather

Every day pictures taken from satellites in space are used to predict the weather. Weather satellites are used to track weather and climate. They follow hurricanes and fires and watch activity from volcanoes. Satellites also spot changes in the ozone layer, the color of the ocean, or the size of ice fields. Satellites help us see how our planet is changing—for better or for worse.

Today our planet continues to grow warmer. The overall temperature of the air is increasing. As a result, water temperatures in the oceans and lakes also rise. Some scientists claim that global warming has already affected our environment, and they predict that rising temperatures will eventually cause serious changes to Earth's delicate balance. Global warming could especially affect the weather with unusual temperatures, severe storms, heavy rainfall, or unexpected droughts.

Droughts are becoming more frequent worldwide and are connected to increasing global temperatures.

Acid Rain

Pollution in our atmosphere can lead to another problem: acid rain. Some pollutants, once they are in the air, produce acid. Then when rain, snow, and fog fall to Earth, the acid is picked up along the way and delivered to Earth. It is called acid rain. The acid settles on trees, plants, soil, water, and even buildings. Acid also travels with the water that runs off into our lakes, rivers, and seas.

Marine life is often the first to show signs of damage from acid rain. Acid rain can kill insects, fish, and plants that live in the water.

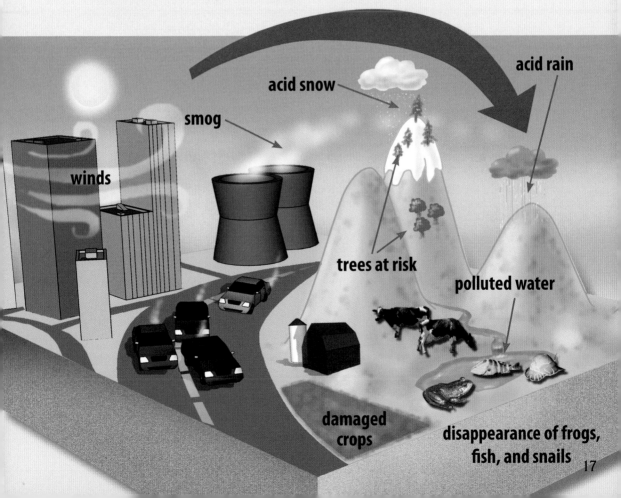

acid rain

acid snow

smog

winds

trees at risk

polluted water

damaged crops

disappearance of frogs, fish, and snails

Deforestation

Deforestation is another way the atmosphere is being damaged. Deforestation happens when large areas of forest are cut down or burned. The land is then used for farms, pastures, or homes.

You might be wondering what trees have to do with the atmosphere. The loss of too many trees can create serious problems. Trees use up carbon dioxide, so fewer trees mean that more carbon dioxide stays in the air. Too much carbon dioxide, a greenhouse gas, can cause more heat to be trapped in the atmosphere. When forests are burned, the smoke sends even more greenhouse gases into the air. Twenty percent of all the greenhouse gases in the atmosphere come from rain forest destruction.

Trees are an important part of a healthy planet. They consume carbon dioxide and give off clean oxygen that we need to breathe. Fewer trees mean less oxygen for living things.

Forests are also important for maintaining moisture in the soil. When it rains, leaves catch water from the air. Tree roots help water soak deep into the ground. Roots, broken branches, and fallen leaves all keep water from running down a slope or hill. When the trees are gone, water just keeps on going, eroding the soil and leaving the area to dry out.

Deforestation affects all parts of the biosphere—the atmosphere, the hydrosphere, and the geosphere.

Hydrosphere: Pure Water for All

The three systems of Earth—atmosphere, hydrosphere, and geosphere—are closely connected. The air affects the water, which affects the soil, and so on.

The hydrosphere is all the water found on, under, and above our planet. The warm air on Earth keeps most water from freezing. The oceans hold 97 percent of Earth's water. The rest is found in rivers, lakes, snow, ice, rain, and clouds. More than 70 percent of Earth's surface is covered with water. Water sets Earth apart from other planets, which do not have a water supply.

Water is what is called a renewable resource—it doesn't get used up. It just keeps moving from the oceans and lakes to the atmosphere, back to the soil and bodies of water. This process is called the water cycle. Because water is part of every system on the planet, it is important to keep our water clean.

A variety of things can change the quality of water. Natural events such as volcanoes, earthquakes, and heavy rain can cause pollution—the contamination of the air, water, or soil with any substance. Human activities can also pollute our waters.

Spreading fertilizers on crops or spraying pesticides can cause problems when they run off into bodies of water. Once in the water, these substances can damage the delicate balance of plant and fish life. Too much fertilizer in a lake can cause plants in the water to grow too rapidly. Widespread plant growth then blocks the sun and oxygen from getting to the fish, causing them to die.

Water is extremely important for maintaining life on Earth. It is an essential natural resource that everyone needs to work to protect.

Lost Beauty

In 1998, the beautiful Rangiroa Atoll coral reefs in French Polynesia died suddenly. Scientists said the reefs died because too much radiation from the sun increased water temperatures for three months—an unusually long period of time. A coral reef is an underwater ridge or mound made up of living coral, coral skeletons, and other living organisms. When these living organisms die, it is referred to as coral bleaching. The coral bleaching at the Rangiroa Atoll reefs was especially severe. More than 99 percent of the fast-growing corals died. Large colonies of slower growing corals also eventually died. Today divers enjoy seeing all the wildlife in the lagoon. But they can also see the damage to the coral reefs.

Earth provides everything we need for survival, including sources of energy. Our geosphere—the soil and rocks on the surface of Earth as well as below—is a rich energy resource. But we need to use what Earth has to offer without damaging the planet in the process.

Fossil fuels such as coal, oil, and natural gas are the most commonly used energy sources today. Fossil fuels were once plants and animals that died and decayed. Over time, the heat and pressure from piles of sediment transformed them. They became a dark substance that eventually broke down into liquid or gas that could be used as fuel. Since they are found underneath the surface of Earth, they must be mined or pumped out of the ground.

Fossil fuels are called nonrenewable fuels. That means that once they are used up, they cannot be

replaced quickly. It took a very long time for decayed plants and animals to turn into usable fuels.

Oil is a valuable source of energy. We use it to drive our cars, heat our homes, and run our factories. But oil is not a clean source of energy. When we use it and other fossil fuels, we are polluting the air. Burning these fuels sends additional greenhouse gases into the air.

There are other sources of energy that we can use. Some, like the sun and wind, are renewable resources. Scientists are working on cleaner energy sources that do not emit pollutants. They are even working on ways to turn water into energy that will power cars. Using alternative forms of energy will help keep our planet healthy.

Wind turbines may provide your power in the future.

Earth is an amazing planet. We all need to work together to make sure it stays clean and healthy. We have a responsibility to take care of the only home we have.

Many individuals, organizations, and countries are working together to care for Earth. Some are trying to fix the damage that has already been done. Others are working to slow down harmful processes that threaten the planet's delicate balance.

All Earth's residents must get involved to keep the planet running smoothly.

In December 1997, the United Nations took action. It held a climate change conference, the first international effort to reduce greenhouse gases in our atmosphere. Some, but not all, countries agreed to what became known as the Kyoto Protocol. They promised to reduce their greenhouse gas emissions. Some nations have been able to keep their promises, but not others. For various reasons, the United States did not ratify, or agree to, the protocol.

Silent Spring

Rachel Carson (1907–1964) was an American marine biologist and writer who took responsibility for caring for the planet, and in doing so, sparked the fire of the environmental movement. Her 1962 book, *Silent Spring*, had a particularly powerful effect. In her book, Carson wrote about the dangers of pesticides, the chemicals used to kill harmful pests and weeds. She explained that the chemicals—especially DDT—were not just destroying pests; they were also harming our environment. She explained how pesticides were harmful to our air and water and were killing fish, birds, and other animals. She thought pesticides also might pose a threat to humans.

A Link in the Chain

Humans are just one link in the chain of nature. When we damage a link, we alter the entire chain. For example, all living things are part of a food web, and each part is closely tied to the others. When part of the web changes, the other parts are affected and become unbalanced. Humans are also part of the food web, and our actions affect other animals. Overfishing salmon, for example, can affect bear populations. A healthy Earth depends on harmony among all the food webs. Humans have the responsibility to protect and preserve other living things.

It's going to take the whole world working together to make lasting changes that will preserve our planet. Part of human responsibility is being careful with Earth's resources. Using renewable sources of energy is one way to help so other energy sources don't run low.

Humans must also be careful what we send into the air or dump on land or in water. If our air, water, and land get too dirty, Earth may not be a safe place to live any longer. And Earth is our only home.

We must also think of new ways to use our resources over and over again. The inhabitants of Earth face a big challenge: to use our resources wisely and make them last a very long time. The choices we make every day affect our planet and its survival.

The average American produces 4.5 pounds (2 kilograms) of trash a day.

Julia Butterfly Hill

On December 10, 1997, a 23-year-old environmentalist named Julia Hill decided to save at least one tree from destruction. That day she climbed up a California redwood tree to prevent loggers from cutting it down. The 600-year-old tree—affectionately called Luna—towered 180 feet (55 meters) into the sky. Hill stayed in Luna for 738 days. That's more than two years. It was the longest anyone had ever lived in a tree.

Hill's mission began when she first traveled to the West Coast of the United States. There she saw people trying to protect the redwood trees from deforestation. The forest used to stretch more than 400 miles (644 km), but now the Pacific Lumber Company was cutting some of it down. Hill joined the fight.

In the end, Hill and the logging company made a deal. Pacific Lumber agreed to leave Luna standing, along with all the trees in a 3-acre (1.2-hectare) area around it. And Hill agreed to come out of the tree. The last part of the deal was controversial. The $50,000 that Hill and other environmentalists had raised for the cause was given to the logging company. Then Pacific Lumber donated the money to a university for research on forestry.

One person can't reverse all the damage done to Earth. So some might say, why bother? But one person can make a difference. And many individuals together can make Earth a cleaner, healthier place to live.

One thing you can do is recycle your soda cans, water bottles, and paper. You can also buy things made from recycled products.

Another thing you can do is find new ways to get from place to place. Could you walk or ride your bike to school? Could you carpool to activities so everyone doesn't have to drive a separate car? All these things will reduce pollution and keep our air cleaner. And since all Earth's systems work together, you'd also be keeping our water and soil cleaner. If all 6 billion people on Earth made better choices every day, we could make a huge difference.

Biking is good for the environment— and it's fun, too!

What's in Your Trash?

Paper products make up about 40 percent of our trash. Americans throw away enough paper each year to build a wall 12 feet (3.6 m) high, stretching from Los Angeles to New York City. Just think what a difference we could make on Earth if everyone recycled all their paper.

Is That A Soda Bottle You're Wearing?

What happens to those plastic soda and water bottles after you drop them into the recycling bin? Some companies turn them into shoes. In 1991, a small company made the first shoe from recycled materials. It used soda bottles, magazines, plastic milk jugs, coffee filters, and much more. This got the attention of some big shoe companies. Now big brands such as Adidas and Nike are trying to find new ways to use recycled material. So when you grow out of your shoes, don't put them in the trash. Shoe companies have also found a way to recycle them—again.

Acid Rain Damage

Many old buildings and statues are made from marble, limestone, or sandstone. These materials have large amounts of calcium carbonate, which is also found in some brands of chalk. The acid in acid rain can wash off part of the surface of buildings made with these materials. It can also cause corrosion on things made of metal, such as cars and bridges. All rainwater is a little bit acidic. However, when rain is very acidic from the effects of pollution, it can do damage. This science activity will use liquids of varying acidity to explore the effects of acid rain on buildings and statues.

Materials

- clear drinking glass
- 6 pieces of chalk (not the dustless type)
- small bowl
- notebook and pencil
- rainwater (leave a dish outside to collect rain)
- vinegar
- clear carbonated drink (lemon-lime soda or sparkling water)
- lemon juice

Procedure

1   Put one piece of chalk in the clear drinking glass. Add rainwater so the chalk is completely covered.

2   Put a second piece of chalk in the small bowl. Add enough vinegar so the chalk is completely covered.

3   Observe both containers of chalk for a few minutes. Note any changes. Then leave them overnight.

4   On day two, record what you see. Do you see any gas bubbles in the glass with chalk and rainwater? Are there any gas bubbles in the bowl with the chalk and vinegar? Where are the bubbles coming from?

Day 2

5   Repeat the activity. This time, instead of vinegar, use lemon-lime soda or sparkling carbonated water (carbonated drinks contain carbon dioxide). On the second day, record your findings. Is the carbon dioxide in the soda or sparkling water enough to break down the chalk?

6   Repeat the activity one more time. This time pour lemon juice over one piece of chalk and vinegar over the other. Observe what happens as the pieces of chalk break down. Higher concentrations of acid cause the chalk to break down faster. What is more acidic—lemon juice or vinegar?

Rachel Carson (1907–1964)
American marine biologist, environmentalist, and writer who helped found the modern environmental movement with the publication of her book *Silent Spring* in 1962

Barry Commoner (1917–   )
American biologist, educator, and environmental activist; outlined the four laws of ecology in his 1971 book, *The Closing Circle*

Paul Ralph Ehrlich (1932–   )
American biologist and educator who first proposed the theory that human survival depends on the realization that Earth's natural resources are nonrenewable and too limited to support the growing population; wrote *The Population Bomb* in 1968

Charles Sutherland Elton (1900–1991)
British environmental scientist who developed in the 1920s the idea that organisms form a pyramid of food levels that keep the energy flow within the ecosystem in balance; at the base are the producers and at the top are herbivores and a small number of carnivores

Aldo Leopold (1886–1948)
American naturalist who was one of the first scientists to arouse public interest in wilderness conservation; wrote *A Sand Country Almanac*

Robert Helmer MacArthur (1930–1972)
American environmental scientist who, along with Edward O. Wilson, wrote *The Theory of Island Biogeography,* which marked the beginning of biogeography, a branch of environmental science that focuses on stable ecological systems

Thomas Robert Malthus (1766–1834)
British economist who wrote some of the earliest
accounts of problems encountered by an expanding
human population

George Perkins Marsh (1801–1882)
American statesman, diplomat, and scholar who is
noted for his pioneering work in the field of conservation

John Muir (1838–1914)
British-born American naturalist who is noted for his work
to gain popular and federal support of forest conservation

Paul Hermann Müller (1899–1965)
Swiss chemist who discovered the effect of the
insecticide DDT; won the Nobel Prize in 1948

Gifford Pinchot (1865–1946)
American public official who made several great
conservation contributions during Theodore Roosevelt's
presidency (1901–1909)

John Wesley Powell (1834–1902)
American geologist, ethnologist, and anthropologist
whose explorations of the United States, especially in
the West, laid the groundwork for numerous federal
conservation projects

Gilbert White (1720–1793)
British naturalist who wrote *The Natural History and
Antiquities of Selborne*, one of the first known works
on ecology

Edward Osborne Wilson (1929–   )
American entomologist, ecologist, and sociobiologist
who, along with Robert H. MacArthur, wrote *The
Theory of Island Biogeography*, which marked the
beginning of biogeography, a branch of ecology that
focuses on stable ecological systems

100	Chinese invent the first insecticide using a powder of dried chrysanthemum flowers
1789	Gilbert White writes the first book on ecology, *The Natural History and Antiquities of Selborne*
1804	Nicholas de Saussure discovers that plants need carbon dioxide from the air and nitrogen from the soil
1879	The U.S. Geological Survey is established
1882	The first hydroelectric plant opens in Wisconsin
1892	John Muir establishes the Sierra Club
1897	Progressive environmentalism, a movement that supports government intervention to modify the exploitation of natural resources by private developers, is established
1898	Rivers and Harbors Act bans pollution of navigable waters in the United States
1908	Chlorination is first used to treat water, making it 10 times purer than when filtered
1933	Civilian Conservation Corps is developed and employs more than 2 million Americans to help in forestry, flood control, and beautification projects around the United States
1935	U.S. Soil Conservation Service is established
1956	Water Pollution Control Act makes federal money available for water treatment plants
1962	Rachel Carson publishes *Silent Spring,* a look at the dangers of the unchecked use of pesticides in nature

1970	First Earth Day is celebrated in the United States; amended Clean Air Act toughens air standards but fails to address acid rain and airborne toxic chemicals
1972	DDT, a pesticide that caused a decline in several bird species, is phased out in the United States; Oregon passes the first bottle recycling law
1974	Arab oil embargo creates an energy crisis in the United States with gasoline and heating oil shortages
1976	Studies show that chlorofluorocarbons from spray cans contribute to the decrease in ozone
1978	People are evacuated from Love Canal, New York, which was discovered to have been a major chemical waste dump
1979	Three Mile Island nuclear power plant in Pennsylvania experiences a near meltdown
1982– 2007	The temperature of Earth's atmosphere rises by at least half a degree
1986	Chernobyl nuclear power plant in the Soviet Union experiences a massive failure, contaminating large areas of the surrounding region and northern Europe
1986– 2007	Major wildfires in the United States increase fourfold
1987	The Montreal Protocol is signed by 24 countries, reducing and eventually phasing out the use of chlorofluorocarbons by the end of the century
1990– 2004	U.S. greenhouse gas emissions increase by 16 percent

1992	Small amounts of ozone depletion are reported for the first time in the Northern Hemisphere
1993	The ozone hole over Antarctica reaches record size, which is thought to be the continuing result of the volcanic eruption of Mount Pinatubo
1997	The United Nations holds a climate change conference, the first international effort to reduce greenhouse gases in our atmosphere; in the resulting Kyoto Protocol, some but not all countries promise to reduce their carbon dioxide emissions
1999	Unusually warm, wet weather allows the West Nile virus to enter the United States
2002	A large section of the Larsen Ice Shelf in Antarctica disintegrates
2005	To date, the hottest year on record worldwide
2007	The United States experiences its largest number of wildfires ever; European Union member countries agree to cut greenhouse gas emissions by 20 percent by 2020
2008	A University of California, Santa Barbara, study of island ecosystems suggests that wildlife diversity is increasing, not decreasing
2012	The Kyoto Protocol is set to expire

acid rain—rain, snow, or fog that contains acids made from pollutants mixing with water in the air

atmosphere—blanket of gases that surrounds a planet

carbon dioxide—gas in the air that animals give off and plants use to make food; greenhouse gas in air that traps heat from the sun

deforestation—cutting down or destruction of forests

energy—source of usable power, such as coal or oil

environment—natural world of land, sea, air, plants, and animals

extinct—no longer existing

food web—multiple food chains connected within an ecosystem

fossil fuels—fuels, including coal, oil, or natural gas, made from the remains of ancient organisms

geosphere—the solid, rocky part of Earth

global warming—rise in the average worldwide temperature of the troposphere

greenhouse gases—any gases in the atmosphere that trap heat from the sun

habitat—where plants or animals live in their natural states

hydrosphere—system made up of all the water on the planet

infrared rays—heat rays; a form of radiation similar to visible light that is given off by all warm objects

natural resources—any substance found in nature that people use, such as soil, air, trees, coal, and oil

ozone layer—layer of the upper atmosphere that absorbs harmful ultraviolet light

pesticides—substances, usually chemical, applied to crops to kill harmful insects and other creatures

pollution—contamination of the soil, water, or atmosphere

radiation—emission of energy waves

recycle—reprocess and reuse old material into a new use or function

sediment—sand, mud, and other particles produced from weathering

stratosphere—layer of the atmosphere above the troposphere, rising up about 31 miles (50 km)

troposphere—layer of the atmosphere closest to Earth, extending 5 to 9 miles (8 to 14.5 km) above the surface

Donald, Rhonda Lucas. *Water Pollution*. New York: Children's Press, 2001.

Miller, Kimberly. *What If We Run Out of Fossil Fuels?* New York: Children's Press, 2002.

Nardo, Don. *Climate Crisis: The Science of Global Warming*. Minneapolis: Compass Point Books, 2008.

Spilsbury, Louise. *Environment at Risk: The Effects of Pollution*. Chicago: Raintree, 2006.

Stille, Darlene R. *The Greenhouse Effect: Warming the Planet*. Minneapolis: Compass Point Books, 2007.

Stille, Darlene R. *Nature Interrupted: The Science of Environmental Chain Reactions*. Minneapolis: Compass Point Books, 2008.

On the Web

For more information on this topic, use FactHound.

1. Go to *www.facthound.com*
2. Choose your grade level.
3. Begin your search.

This book's ID number is 9780756540708

FactHound will find the best sites for you.

Index

Gina Dal Fuoco

Gina Dal Fuoco has been a teacher for 12 years. She was born and raised near the California coast. Living near the ocean helped develop her curiosity about all the various species that live underwater. She enjoys learning about these creatures while living in California with her husband and two children.

Image Credits